IF FOUND, PLEASE FILL OUT ONE PAGE
OF YOUR CHOOSING AND THEN CONTACT:

_____

_____

_____

_____

THANK YOU, KIND STRANGER!

SKEDADDLE

An Out-There TRAVEL JOURNAL

By Karina Portuondo
and Travis Nichols

CHRONICLE BOOKS
SAN FRANCISCO

ISBN: 978-1-4521-7042-8

Manufactured in China.

MIX
Paper from
responsible sources
FSC™ C136333

Design by Kayla Ferriera

10 9 8 7 6 5 4 3 2 1

Chronicle Books LLC
680 Second Street
San Francisco, California 94107

www.chroniclebooks.com

CONTENTS

How to use this **JOURNAL**

Skedaddle is for recording all the things that make a trip weird, wonderful, and one of a kind.

The prompts in these pages will guide you to write, list, and doodle about magical moments, minor misfortunes, and everything in between. Consider this a freestyle journal—flip to any page and fill 'er up as you go (or even when you're back home). Dedicate the entire thing to one special trip, or pop in and out over the course of a few. Maybe recruit your fellow travelers to pitch in. There's no right way to *Skedaddle*, so do whatever your wandering heart desires. Whether you're backpacking for the better part of a year, taking your annual family vacay, or going on a quick group getaway, use *Skedaddle* to document time well spent. Later on, you can reminisce about those fleeting feelings, little lessons, and meaningful memories.

`Happy travels!`

FOR the RECORD

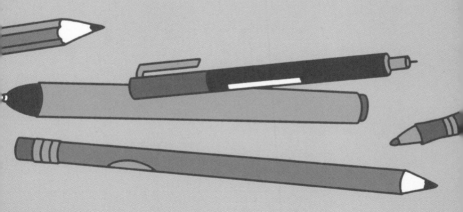

Useful **GEAR**

Handy dandy doodads.

Useless **JUNK**

Needed the kit, but not the caboodle.

Stubs & Stuff

Tix or it didn't happen.

TAPE MEMENTOS HERE OR STASH
THEM IN THE BACK POCKET.

Travel ENEMIES

Just the worst.

FAVORITE **STRANGERS**

Bestie potential.

\# OF DOGS PET

Local STYLE

Notable fashion statements.

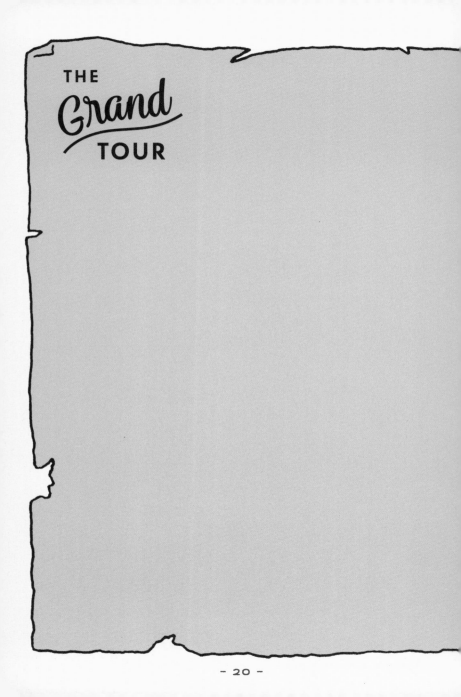

THE

Grand

TOUR

DRAW A MAP OF THE JOURNEY.

BIG **FIRSTS**

Standing ovation-worthy stuff.

DEFINITE LASTS

Never again. **Never.**

ACCIDENTAL *Adventures*

EMERGENCY Errands

FORGOT *to* PACK

<Facepalm.gif>

LOST Forever

Atlantis. Blackbeard's treasure. A single sock.

Natural WONDERS

1.

2.

3.

4.

5.

6.

7.

Manmade WONDERS

1.

2.

3.

4.

5.

6.

7.

Cultural MISUNDERSTANDINGS

Eeeeeeeesh.

CUSTOMS **COMPREHENDED**

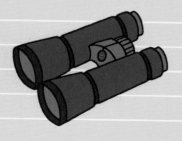

Overheard

FUNNY SIGNS & *Odd Ads*

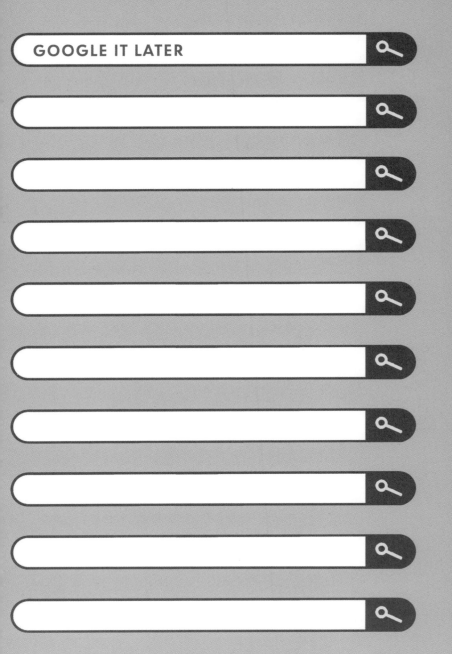

GOOGLE IT LATER

FOOD *Peaks*

FOOD Fails

Food, meet napkin. Napkin, meet pocket.

Experience	NOTES
	RATING ☆☆☆☆☆
	☆☆☆☆☆
	☆☆☆☆☆
	☆☆☆☆☆
	☆☆☆☆☆
	☆☆☆☆☆

Experience	NOTES
	RATING ☆☆☆☆☆
	☆☆☆☆☆
	☆☆☆☆☆
	☆☆☆☆☆
	☆☆☆☆☆
	☆☆☆☆☆

lo·cal lin·go noun \ lō-kəl liŋ-(,)gō\ : words and phrases used by residents of a particular place

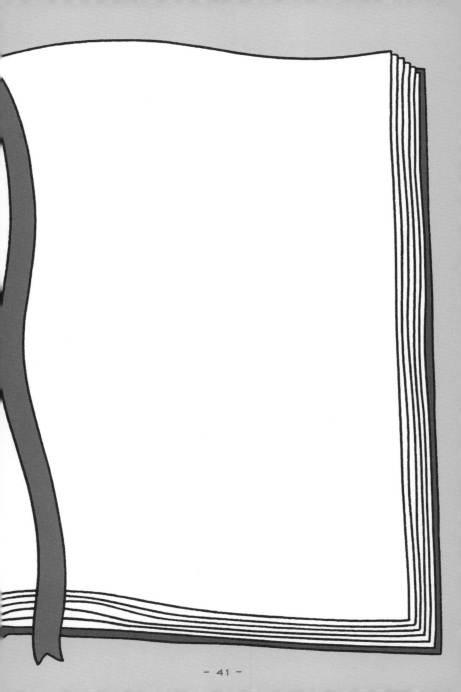

SAFETY CONCERNS

That was **not** OK.

RULES *Broken*

Chuck caution directly into the wind's stupid face.

Cloudspotters Club

DRAW OR DESCRIBE WHAT YOU SEE IN THE SKY

Stargazers Society

STELLAR SKETCHES GO HERE

RESTROOM Adventures

Toilet-related tales.

THE **HYGIENE** SITUATION

That fresh and clean (or not) routine.

QUOTES & *Inside* JOKES

ABSOLUTE LOW POINTS

Rock bottom.

Best LIFE MOMENTS

Crushin' it. Killin' it. Winning. Blessed. #otherhashtags.

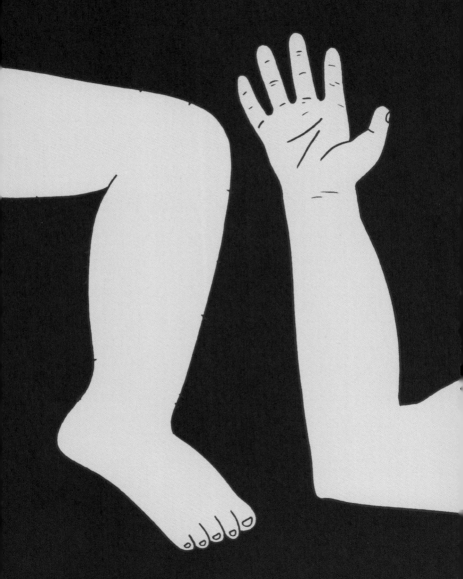

SOUVENIR TRACKER

Gift	Giftee

Best PURCHASE(S)

What a gem.

BUYER'S **REMORSE**

Regret it? Don't sweat it!

NEWLY DISCOVERED **STRENGTHS**

AREAS *for* IMPROVEMENT

YOU'LL
GET
THERE

Found Flora

PRESS OR TRACE FLOWERS
AND LEAVES HERE.

Standout STATUES

TREES *to* REMEMBER

STRESS City

Can't. Even.

Super CHILL

Relaxed to the max.

MYTHS & LEGENDS **LEARNED**

Creatures & Ghost STORIES

New **SNACKS & DRINKS**

Eating this forever now, thanks.

NEW **GAMES** & **THINGS**

Bonus: No one lost an eye.

Cute KIDS

From the mouths of babes.

Admirable **ELDERS**

Wisdom galore.

HEALTH-RELATED Happenings

Alive, but not exactly kicking.

Physical **FITNESS**

Pretty much an Olympian.

THE **BORING** BITS

Zzz, amirite?!

Adrenaline RUSHES

Lifestyle: EXTREME.

LESSONS *Learned*

Guess we'll have to go back!

What'll Be **MISSED**

Why don't we have this at home?

FUN FACTS *Found Out*

-
-
-
-
-
-
-
-

BOREDOM
BUSTERS

10 THINGS TO TRY:

☐ Send a postcard.

_____

_____

☐ Support a small business.

_____

_____

☐ Throw a coin into a fountain.

_____

_____

☐ Listen to live music.

_____

_____

☐ Take a local's recommendation.

_____

_____

Beginner 👑

☐ Relax under a tree.

_____

_____

☐ Take a shortcut.

_____

_____

☐ Treat yourself to something special.

_____

_____

☐ Visit a body of water.

_____

_____

☐ Learn the name of a new plant.

_____

_____

10 THINGS TO TRY:

☐ Dance with a stranger.

_____

_____

☐ Use a fake name for a day.

_____

_____

☐ Play an instrument.

_____

_____

☐ Leave a positive review.

_____

_____

☐ Have a home-cooked meal.

_____

_____

Advanced

☐ Sneak in somewhere.

_____

_____

☐ Take a 5-hour break from your phone.

_____

_____

☐ Haggle for something.

_____

_____

☐ Wear a makeshift costume.

_____

_____

☐ Spot a wild animal.

_____

_____

Dueling Dots

Take turns connecting 2 dots (no diagonals). When you complete a square, put your initial in it and go again. Whoever gets the most squares at the end is the winner.

WHERE'RE THOSE
WORDS AT?!

```
K S W K W R L A P L T H
E J T I C E E A D E R I
P A F R Z A S D E B R D
E I D Z E S P F N E W D
S S G A P E T K V A M E
O O C P E T O C A W N
O T R O E T Y D R A Q G
M T D R O A E C O B B E
A I T S L T S R U G S M
V S K E D A D D L E Q M
R E D N O W B V N N T B
```

PASSPORT	LAYOVER	LEZZGO
BACKPACK	ADAPTER	SCRAM
SKEDADDLE	HIDDEN GEM	WANDER
STREET FEET	VAMOOSE	WONDER
STREET DOG	WIFI	SCOOT

I SPY SOMETHING . . .

Triangular	
RUSTY	
Shiny	
SPOOKY	
Adorable	
SKETCHY	
Tawdry	
BORING	
Heartwarming	
FILTHY	

	PECULIAR
	Cold
	TINY
	Radiant
	Unassuming
	Fancy
	MAJESTIC
	SURPRISING
	Bumpy
	FLUFFY

VAGABOND *Bingo*

Human statue	FULL BAND	BEACH GLASS	*Magician*	Gift shop
BROKEN TILE	Bucket Drummer	*Sunrise*	FOOT-PRINTS	FANCY FOOD TRUCK
Rain	SNOWY PEAK	★	Juggler	SCARY BUG
Bad Street Art	*Unicyclist*	BRIDGE	FANNY PACK	Celebrity
ORION'S BELT	Runner	*Older couple*	PAINTER	FRUIT TREE

GO FOR FIVE IN A ROW.

MISCELLANEOUS NOTES

CONVERSIONS *Cheat Sheet*

The numbers below are ROUNDED to help you do some quick mental math and get the gist.

WHEN YOU'RE ON YOUR WAY

1 inch ≈ 2.5 centimeters	1 meter ≈ 1 yard
1 foot ≈ .3 meters	10 meters ≈ 11 yards
10 feet ≈ 3 meters	10 kilometers ≈ 6 miles
10 miles ≈ 16 kilometers	50 kilometers ≈ 31 miles
50 miles ≈ 80 kilometers	100 kilometers ≈ 60 miles

When you're weighing your options

1 ounce ≈ 30 grams	1 stone ≈ 14 pounds
2 pounds ≈ 1 kilogram	100 grams ≈ 3.5 ounces
100 pounds ≈ 45 kilograms	100 kilograms ≈ 220 pounds
1 pint ≈ .5 liters	1 liter ≈ 2 pints
½ gallon ≈ 2 liters	4 liters ≈ 1 gallon

IN

When you're asked about the weather

30° F ≈ -1° C

50° F ≈ 10° C

70° F ≈ 21° C

90° F ≈ 32° C

110° F ≈ 43° C

When you walk through your shoes while walking the earth

US (W)	US (M)	UK	EUR	Mondo
5	4	3	35	220
6	5	4	36.5	230
7	6	5	37.5	235
8	7	6	39	245
9	8	7	40	255
10	9	8	41.5	265
11	10	9	42.5	270
12	11	10	44	280
13	12	11	46.5	295

CM

Karina Portuondo and *Travis Nichols* have traveled together through over 25 countries on 6 continents . . . so far. They've explored by air and sea, rail and bus, balloon and squeaky bike, and on both sides of the street. Karina and Travis have (supposedly mandatory) international driver's licenses and yellow fever vaccination certificates that they've weirdly never had to show to anyone. They live in San Francisco with a dog who has only barked at a TSA agent once.

LEZZGO!

Greetings from OUT HERE

where to?

VACATION FOREVER

SKEDADDLE

yONDER

GO GO GO GO GO GO GO GO GO GO

fold the tops of these sticky bookmarks over your favorite pages